Poetry collection

Gloaming Reveries

Poetry collection

Gloaming Reveries

Jenny Hu

July 2023

*For my loving husband Xuyu
and my daughters Angel and Olivia*

Acknowledgment

I am grateful to my English teacher Megan who has been teaching and giving feedback in my writings. To many different people whom I met in poetry group for inspiration, encouragement and discussion. To my beloved family, my husband Xuyu for being a constant and untiring audience and my daughters Angel and Olivia for their lovely illustrations to embellish those stances. And special thanks to my publisher (Publishing Push London) who have transformed my writings into a printed book.

Contents

Proem

Poetry has always possessed a special place in my heart. When I was a little girl, I remember my grandma telling me that a good child should love to read. She should hold the memory of what she had read so she wouldn't fail her exams, then she can go to university, and have a good education and a good life. Reading and memorising those classical Chinese poems such as "Three Hundred Tang Poems Collection" was a must-do homework for me and so it was for most if not every child at that time. Reciting was already inked into a child's daily life. For example, poems by Li Bai have been committed to memory since I was about the age of going to nursery, such as this one: " The bright moonlight at my bedside/ would it be frost on the ground/I raise my head gazing at the bright moon/lower down I miss my hometown". (床前明月光/疑是地上霜/举头望明月/低头思故乡).

After all these years, I hadn't become a poet. Instead, I became a scientist, dedicating most of my life to the research of the biology of cancer, and raising my family. However, a connection to poetry, the image of that special voice has been planted deep in my heart. Apart from those ancient Chinese poets, throughout time, the English poets also came into my life freely and voluntarily: William Shakespeare, Emily Bronte, Elizabeth Browning, Emily Dickens, Keats, Shelley, Dylan Thomas, Robert Frost, William Wordsworth and many more. Yet, I still remember my grandma's fair smile and her words that meant I wanted to follow my dream. Today, in spite of being old enough to be a grandmother myself, I have decided to refine and record my life experiences and thoughts in the language of English, and poetry seems to be the best tool when I'm gradually rolling into the practice of such an attempt.

Poetry, to me, infuses modern cognition with ancient wisdom. Its lyrical and philosophical aesthetics brings immeasurable pleasure and potent calmness that has helped me to go through my life with celestial strength and courage, especially on those days in which life seems to be gloomy and strained. Writing poetry is not a sudden moment of epiphany; it is the accumulation and precipitation of time and consciousness. Poetry is our eternal comfort and companion. As human beings, we are bestowed with the gift of feeling and ability to express it in words, images and many forms of creative art. In the age of artificial intelligence, it is vitally important that we don't lose this special gift of humanity, indeed at a spiritual level.

To those who still read poetry today and who especially have chosen to read this poetry collection, let me quote a lovely poem "The Gardener" by Rabindranath Tagore:

> Who are you, reader, reading my poems an hundred years hence?
> I cannot send you one single flower from this wealth of the spring

4

One single streak of gold from yonder clouds
Open your doors and look abroad.

From your blossoming garden gather fragrant
memories
Of the vanished flowers of an hundred years before
In the joy of your heart may you feel the living joy
That sang one spring morning, sending its glad
voice
Across an hundred years.

Readers, you're the interesting souls among the many
thousands of all.

Jenny Hu
07/07/2023

1. Home

When I was a little girl, I had my house key
Slung around my neck, every day after school
I walked briskly back to the familiar dwelling,
I knew was my home.

When I'd grown up, I left
And flew far away from the familiar nest.
Home is faded away in the memories
And away those days in rain and shine.

Today I sit peacefully by my own hearth,
Logs burn with the sound of earthly lilt
In lieu of recalling the bustling past,
Much happiness and calmness surround me.

No need for home to be an opulent house,
Something endearing lasts ever more.

6

Those tears and laughs we shared
Have disagreed but never disliked.

Home, regardless of abundant or absent
Freely we live our true selves,
In this love-bearing nest, together
To see the most reassuring scenery.

2. Would you believe?

If I told you, there was a true existence of
Time and space with more than three dimensions,
But you could only see when you
Throw yourself into the misty world
Breaking through the grey glass
Dancing along with the twinkling stars,
Would you believe?

If I told you, one day you will enchant
A dreaming space under the moonlight,
Despite the recluse and darkness
Your heart filled with joys, like a fawn
Under this endless darkness, a bliss of
Solitude flashing upon you with plenitude,
Would you believe?

8

Following your heart
For the peace and confidence it holds.
Touching the time space from which
Unicorn is calling upon your deep vein,
Please, please, believe in you.

3. Hope

Hope is a pair of eyes, even in the gutter
Look up by the starlight,
Across the vast wilderness
Of deep dark cave,
Search for a distant star.

Hope is the moss of flower, in the swamp
Although the haze casts desolation,
Torrential rain makes wetlands muddy,
But the moss of flower
Still growing steadfastly.

Hope is a reed, inhabited by a soul
In the darkness, the feeble thing
Waiting for the morning's dew,
When the sun rises, its awakening
Like a plump bird ready, flying afar.

4. Summer stroll under the Magdalen Bridge

Summer stroll under the Magdalen Bridge
The stream of river Cherwell lingers around.
Babbling water reflects the tint glowing of image
Summer stroll under the Magdalen Bridge.

Sunset paints the golden hue on the wall of college,
Laughter's immersed in the boat docking sound,
Summer stroll under the Magdalen Bridge
The stream of river Cherwell lingers around.

5. Birds

On the branch of a willow trunk
Stood a pair of tweeting singers.
Preening their feathers,
Flipping each other's wings.
A couple of young darlings, I think
Searching for dwelling,
In this yelling, hailing day.

From a distance, I saw them and they saw
Me too, but the drenched couple didn't
Entreat to enter my garden door.
From the nothingness they leap
Both pick up on each other's gaze,
They flipped and flitted,
In this yelling, hailing day.

6. The moon is a hesitant flake

The moon is a hesitant flake,
Falls into my favourite lake
Swimming as if a white dove,
Filled with forever joy of love
And fear not to make a mistake.

The night is embraced with darkened break,
All the creatures yet to be wide awake
Air emanated with petrichor of dried clove,
The moon is a lonely, white, ancient warrior.

The buckwheat flower flying like a snowflake,
A panicked magpie flaps his wings to escape,
Morning dew shines aloft of grove
Before the wilderness starts to rove.
The last silver lines spread alike an arrow break,
The moon is a solemn ship ready, for sailing away.

7. To my dahlia

Deep autumn is touching my fingers
Sunset paints the garden a golden hue, lightly
The chrysanthemums are swaying in the wind.

There are arrays of dahlia, red and dark purple
Flying proudly in the breeze, slightly raised petals
As if chanting to the moonlight when dusk falls.

Carefully, I covered their roots with grated pinewood
For the euphoric petals rather shiver in the cold wind
Than decorating the vase for the sake of cosiness.

8. Bubbles

Three bubbles
Huge, empty, frothy
Rising from the dusty lands
A giant, clings to direly
Seeing a mirage.

9. The lady locked in sorrow

She was once cordially called "heaven's pride",
For she ever had a good and natural smile.
Searching for her dreams, she patched up fear,
Enduring her deceased mother's words,
Her life may have appeared all fine fair,
Until one day, she was shrouded in sorrow.

Far away the barren land was immersed in sorrow,
Few lives in the light and rare walks of pride.
Folks noised for carnival at an unheard fair,
The dirt pleasure trod upon the innocence of smile,
The man's beastly grasp drowned out the words,
And the damsel shattered in a poignant fear.

She wept and drifted out to an isolated fear,
Could anyone hear her long sigh of sorrow?
Odd micro lens captured her muttered words,
As if she sheltered in a delusion of pride.

Reliving in yesterday's warmness of smile,
She dreamed wandering freely at the fair.

The idiots go round and round at the chaotic fair,
Bustling market was no way to ease her fear.
Kindred villains grin at each other with the wanton smile,
No good morrow, ev'ry day wakes up in wistful sorrow.
Face yellowed, hair greyed, kneeled heart had no pride,
Bleeding voice bellowed out her soundless words.

Her sobs uprisen by the reaper's stabbing words,
The attendant horror covered under the filthy fair.
Her disdainful next of kin took corruptive pride,
Crashing her lowness to the ground of infinite fear.
Her premature wrinkles flecked with dazed sorrow,
In years to please the brutes by her meek smile.

The dark dank cave-like shelter prisoned her smile,
Nonchalantly chill, north-west wind froze her words.
No amount of children can save her from sorrow,

17

Let alone the ungrateful sons indulged in open fair,
Chains on the nape, a revelation of direful fears.
Run, lady, take hold freely of the dream and pride.

Time to reinstall smile, benevolence prevails with fair,
Plant the seed of truthful words, for fear it may lose,
Nothing lasts forever, neither sorrow nor pride.

10. Fight for your homeland

When the cannonballs rumbled at dawn in the distant
    glen
The enemy's tanks rolled over the black earth like
    serpents
Fight, fight for ev'ry inch of your homeland like
    lunatic men.

The enemies of cowardice hidden under the mounds of
    den
Baffling in inexplicable direction without knowing the
    purpose
When the cannonballs rumbled at dawn in the distant
    glen.

People awakened by the sound of the cannon kept as
    calm as Zen
Even the old grannies willing to defend with their bare
    hands
Fight, fight for ev'ry inch of your homeland like
    lunatic men.

The reckless smoke pervaded and troopers tossed in
    again and again
Wild fang went howling under the moon on this vast
    expanse of land
When the cannonballs rumbled at dawn in the distant
    glen.

People there are experiencing the hardship to their
    most withstand
Whatever difficulty they followed on the commands.
Fight, fight for ev'ry inch of your homeland like
    lunatic men.

Unwavering belief in the prevailing of justice never
    beyond my ken
This is the time; up and fight to defend your
    motherland
When the cannonballs rumbled at dawn in the distant
    glen.
Fight, fight for ev'ry inch of your homeland like
    lunatic men.

11. If

If the sky draws its dark curtain down,
Wrap yourself up and stay calm;
If speak out drown in the tetchy town,
Fill your paper with breath of fresh balm.

If the world is going to be a wolf,
Neither fear nor yowl can turn it round.
Show your courageous face to proof
Of man's last hope can stand on this ground.

Don't be lured only by booze and prom,
Hold steady soberness worthy your conscience;
If you have a goal in mind, despite the storm,
Light in your heart be your own navigation.

Don't believe the grass is greener on the other bank,
After all, you're the one to bridle your own voyage

12. Cat story

I have a cat called Mimi, simple and honest,
He is the one who attracts so many fond thoughts.
When he passed by a pond,
He was shocked by his own reflection.
When he was patted,
He purred as loud as a motor engine.
If he was hungry, he'd miaow tirelessly,
If he was shuttered outside the door,
His yelling sounded like thunder's rumble.
Through the glass door
He waves his furry melon paws
As if a formidable jousting fighter.
Sometimes he howls out of blue, but
Even mad, he is still agreeably cute.

13. For the memory of past emptiness

When the confinement bell knelled, all folks
Halt and flop, in no time super-malls grazed,
Doors sealed; the solemn moon hung over
The featureless vast city, fears shrouded
On masses, muffled in terrifying unknowns.

Countless cameras recorded the extraordinary videos
They've gone viral on social media but soon taken down.
Some shown old men were shoved down on the ground,
Writhed in agonising pain, those innocent cats and dogs
Were captured and taken down, mankind gone mad.

Those unsolicited officers either block the passage
Or break into the private dwellings in the name of
Preventing the spreading of the virus, their bullhorns
Yelling for people to join in the long grave queue
In this miserable bleak wintery day and night.

24

Many mornings, men woke up with the vacant inside
The rumbling sound though you couldn't really hear
But It was as sharp as a needle, pierces
Through craving souls, the silent sobbing
Revolved above the vast void of emptiness.

14. Rousham Garden

William Kent was a genius; his masterpiece
Lay in the embrace of the Oxfordshire countryside.
English greens stretch on the wavy hills, endless
Wonderful trees rustle in the lush waterside
Three hundred years of elegance, timeless.

Emerald Rousham, every shade is green -
The light is green, the pond is green,
Even the unexpected breeze is green.
River Cherwell flows by the fresh meadow
White swan roams freely in the water, tender.

The surprise beauty to me was the handsome
Roosters and hens, so happily, loudly, and yet
Sensibly took a leisurely walk on the open lawn.
The cocks crowing, hens clucking
Birds aloft, formed a united happy chorus.

15. My tribute to the Queen

That later afternoon, when the news broke
Heart broken, couldn't believe that
Our beloved Queen had passed away like a fairy.
Only a few days ago, I saw you on TV,
Your touching smile likes a kindle of light
With you, the world is warmth and harmony.
I gazed up to the north, a magic brilliant flare
Zooming across the ocean and mountains
An extraordinary grace, almighty defender
Beneath the faith, we follow behind you,
A beautiful forgiving mind, noble lily of ascending soul,
This is your eternal happiness, beside your beloved ones
Her majesty, sending darling blessings upon us, forever.

16. When the Scottish bagpipe's calling

When that Scottish bagpipe's calling,
The melodious music, piercing through
The tranquil solemn sky, tuned melancholy
I knew, so do millions there,
This is a moment, heaven's door opens,
Welcoming an elegant beauteous soul home.

My thought is with the royal family, that
Over the past numerous years, I'm proud
Of living in this free and civilised land.
Thanks to her majesty's rules and laws
With which our values defended, no matter
You're rich or poor, pampered or ignored.

Till death, you departed from earthly mundanity.
I believe, in heaven all souls'd be redeemed eternally.

17. City foxes

City foxes, elude in a dank night.
Tired and craving for food, the skulks
Snuffle out urban humpty-dumpty,
Heart-wrenching crying for a bite
Those once easy reach belt.

When the dawn is falling, dusk rose.
A dispirited couple, under the shadow of tree
Between the cliff of walls and street detritus.
Mistook a black swath as a hazel grouse
Calling in vain for a heartbroken companion.

18. The moment of storm

A terrible storm rages on a desolate savanna,
There was unrest between marsh and highland.
An old man wandered around in the storm;
His mind swaying from one whim to another
His lament fixated by his chaos, callously
Raving storm drowned his panting steps.

The wind battered, the rain drenched,
He wobbled down to the loneliness
Whence he'd come, such commiserating
Blurred into the sameness of forbearance.
To the rain, wind, thunder and lightning.
He owes them nothing and vice versa,
Let the storm hit harder and louder
It's glorious in his moment kind of grace.

19. **Old bookstore**

An old bookstore dwells on the corner of the street,
Silently witnesses each and every passing by
For over a half century long of flowing feet
Eager not to fail those minds of quest.

I pushed the door entering an outpost of a paradise,
My imaginary misery suspended in this free small
    world;
Old books charmingly clattered on the time-polished
    shelves
To support each other's steadfast upright.
Some are motley heaped on the rattling ground
    welcoming
Every intrigued bookworm open them with delight.

What a moment when I spot old books otherwise
    nowhere to be found
Like a lost jewel glowing from the forgotten drawer
Inhale the history, smell of yesterday, curiosity
    rebound,
Those long-gone stories returned from ashore.

20. When I'm old

Now I'm old, wrinkled and grey,
Feel weary, sometimes sight's blurry;
Can't see further, surroundings
Seem to have become more disquiet.
Already yield to the things of youth,
Still unwilling to give up my word.

Though I'm old, my spine is bent,
Varicose veins crawl over the legs;
And what hasn't been broken
Was a delicate pearl, buried deep
In the heart, aspire for breathing,
Move forward, yet pace stumbling.

Much land have I crossed, and much distance
Has parted, here I am, with much serenity.

21. Of early autumn

In a wonderful misty morning,
Robin sits on the copper beech branch.
That's his branch, never quitting for his return.
Southern wind gently sweeps over, and
The fallen leaves have flown, some clinch,
As if they hark at each other's longing.

The clouds are whiter and layered,
Day and sun on rising to shine its warmth.
The vigorous summer blooms are bearing fruits,
Salute with mature bend to the calm north
Filled your heart with sweetness to the bay.
Who can refuse to have a toast on this day?

22. Autumn night

Autumn night, high and deep,
Countless stars twinkle one after another.
Spread the shining frost on the locus below,
Most of the flowers tired and faded.
A small hexagon pink still blossom,
Dreams shyly in this cold night.

A nocturnal bird flies overhead,
To a distant wood looking for its resting nest.
Under the eaves of the stone hut,
The grapevines dispersed from frost to frost
To wake up the fallen leaves
Dancing along the path in this ancient town.

23. Evening walk in oak woods

I walked into the southern England woodlands,
Twilight glens on the hilly path beneath my steps.
Feeling the touch of evening dew,
Dripping 'cross the newly born leaves,
I touched it, and the tiny water balls
Shone colourful hues like an enchanting jasper.

And then, when the twilight fell, listen, the quietness,
The peace of it all, that little avenue with the damp mist.
Imagine it became an infinite blue sea to the right,
And an endless brown shore to the left,
Nearby clusters of silhouettes of oak trunks, against
The glowing golden light from the woodlands afar.

24. Seven pillars of wisdom

A woman is building her house
She dug out seven pillars
On which her sheltered dwelling shall set.

First, in awe of the nature's law,
The beginning of the foundation
Of the complex, shall be kept in mind.

Pursue excellence with your loving
Avid heart, no harm to your neighbours
And pass by, this is a second prerequisite.

Take charge of your own decision
Making with responsibilities and
Considerations to your words and actions.

Then come to the terms of tolerance
And humbleness, open-minded with caution
Commiseration cannot be tainted without boundaries.

Being compassion and empathy
Is not the sign of weakness, but
Don't give in your ground of self-defending.

Unwavering in the commitment
With fairness, justice and impartiality
No matter how hard it will be.

Life is art, its property comes from
One's inner peace and strength
Guard it with sanity, destroy it with madness.

Last but not least, uphold the truth
Living with integrity and sincerity
So you value the abode you did up.

Wisdom does not fall from the sky,
It shall be the blossom in our hearts.

25. Let's see the sea

When summer is gone,
Let's see the sea,
For I can still feel it
In the rocky soft breeze.

When autumn is deep,
Let's see the sea,
The last golden glow
Dazzling on the open vase.

When the night is falling,
Let's see the sea,
The rising bright moon
Telling me you're not far.

When the first daylight breaks,
Let's see the sea,
The virile beauty of the light
Like a sword on a warrior's chest.

26. This morning is windier

This morning is windier,
The branches are whiffing louder,
The petals are kissing the ground,
The russet leaves sway without border.

The breeze ruffles meadow grasses,
The clouds are hesitating if not
To give way to a blue yonder.
Only the two indomitable red robins
Ardently guard their newly-wed abode.

27. When Mimi sits beside me

When Mimi sits beside me,
The world is meek and cool;
Sun shines through the magnolia tree
Filling the room with golden green light;
The tapping sound of the branches
Rapping windows, melodious rhythm
Gently hypnotises both Mimi and me.

28. The garden in early October morning

It's windy early morning in October,
Sky looks ominous, rain in waiting;
Lacecap hydrangea, purple and pink
Fluttering in the wind, soft and graceful.
The brugmansia trumpets, saggy yellow
In calling, dare not to act rashly.

Iresine done very well, silky crimson leaves
Hold the morning dew at bay;
Happy carmen, the dwarf canna,
Are you made from the blood
Of Buddha's toes? Glorious touch
Preserved in your many years to come.

The dahlia border still flowering,
Blooming one after another;
Moon fire has been lit since

The first frost of last summer.
Despite the sparsity of the flowers,
Their strengths are still immense.

Clematis goes on far and higher,
Like its name, iron wire connects
Countless blooming purple or white
Relentlessly hold on in the wind;
Those have bloomed, even the deadheads
Don't want to fall into the muddy ground.

With the arrival of frosty winter,
Time to test the cold endurance of them.
Lying still under the sand ground
Perfectly fine, even snowman in check.
But I don't do faffing, no disturbing,
Being a slacker and let nature be nature.

29. A Welsh folk tale for October

I was enchanted by a mythical tale
About these Welsh rosy apples
Turned out to have such charming marks.
There was once a small island
Called Avalon, floating on the northern
Welsh bay with lush apple trees stand
On the gateway to this enchanting fairy land.
A wicked wizard called Merlin lived
In a magical glass castle; he no doubt
Attracted many followers, among such were
Morgan the enchantress healer, and earnest
Half-sister of King Arthur. They admired
His super abilities in prophecy,
Shapeshifting and amazing sagacity.
One day, after a fierce battle, wounded
Morgan brought back his dying king.
Merlin laid him to rest on the hillside
Where many gnarled apple trees were planted.

46

Many years later, people are amazed
To see that these apples are the most
Aromatic and healthy ones among many more.
They believe it is this covert magic sod
Nurturing the ancient Welsh apples
Growth generation after generation.

30. Soul cake

And now I'm making a soul cake
With my children, we're having fun;
Flour, sugar and mixing of eggs,
An apple, a pear and a little pinch
Of nutmeg, any good things
That make us all cheery.

The sun is going down and
The lane is quieter, clock ticks,
Time slows, old chapters return;
When the doorbell rings
One for you, two for her, delightful,
No matter thin or thick of the slice.

31. To my invisible father

Last night I had a dream,
It was a wayward little dream.
In a cold dead heap of haystack
Mischievous feeling of being lost,
A giant black silhouette loomed.

Don't want to be spoiled
At this consummate hour.
Distance made us become strangers;
Completeness is absent at
This enormity of a moment.

32. Story

I came across a fashionable chopstickal novel
A friend of mine talked about with great relish;
But I am faint to listen, not because I'm chondral,
Nor for that I am too old for a romance to cherish.

Think not of them, for how frivolousness that I saw
A disguise of the story was made up to cue;
That the degree of deformity, absurdity and outlaw
Of human being in an overbearing land, is due.

How disparate the world we are living. One's reef
To other's hull, but stories have power to entice,
To instil, illusionary fantasies oust one's belief
Heart-sickening, the story, crouching on populace.

I became a lonely traveller, often rest my mind
On these atilt, sallow shaky stems bearing no fruit.

33. An old lady

Once on a dusky autumn evening,
I met a lady, dragging her large grocery sack.
She walked warily on a narrow pebble lane,
The breeze ruffled her hair, and scarf
Around her neck was blown up in the air
Like a small red carp wagging its tail.
The trailer's wheels hit the gravel ground
A dull sound echoed in the empty street.
I paused and saluted her endeavours.
As if for fear of treading on me, she halted.
Towards me, she smiled dearly.
I returned a greeting sight, "Do you need help?"
"Oh, no," she replied with affable wittiness.
"I am ninety-two years old, but I'm with my liver".
I was caught off guard that she would give me this answer
-
Really in this moment I found a luminary path beside her.

34. Autumn song

Summer flowers in autumn
Still blooming their beauty;
I see a sound,
Yellow cocktail waltz,
Blue indigo jazz,
Sway in this melancholic season.

35. First frost

Season walks into marsh, mist and
Monsoon rains, the lanes are gnawed.
By the frost, the grass crisped;
The estate afar looks immaculate,
Untouched. Under the foot,
The sycamore leaves have gag bear's hue.

The fine moon brightly cut out the sky
On the other side only a few inches.
Above the horizon is the pale sun
Nearly derelict in the countryside.
Silent other than the sound of owl
Echoing the night hymn in the woods.

36. The will of the werewolves

I knew you've been struggling and swaying
Between non-werewolf and werewolf.
It is now the full moon rises,
Time for you to tear off the clothes,
Remould your fingers and arms
Into claws and front legs, with which
You can smear the horrors and fears
With thick fur if you wish.

Last night I saw the lycanthropy happened
Like I watched a scary movie rented many
Years ago, I kept watching until I couldn't
Bear to watch any more. The beaming muscles
Around your muzzle reminded me of the fiercest
Bite that masticates so many innocent lives.
I shuddered with sorrow more than horror;
That one day you may want to turn back
But it will probably be too late.

37. In a green and pleasant land

In a green and pleasant land, I wandered
Freely accompanied by the soft breeze,
Such a golden light lead on to a golden day.
Flicks flock of birds fly under the blue sky
Painted forests stand layer after layer from afar,
Every side of me befalling iridescent sheen.
On the vast hilly grassland, cattle and sheep
Graze down, that beauty and affluence of cultivation
Of nature flips with every pulse of love
And peace, this moment of enjoyment refines
The existence of human being, that replenishes
My heart with fulfilling joy and placidity.
Nothing to compare the sheer purity and peculiarity
With the green grassland that I march on.

38. Then and now

Then you're young —they want you older,
Now you're old—they want you young.
When she's gone— you wish you'd call her back,
When she's back—you hold your lung.

Then you're remote —it's "Hey, I'm coming,"
Now you're tired—still "Sure, let's party,"
When you're down—as if tide receding,
When you frown—she hums a little sobbing.

Then you're poor—it's time to leave the shelf,
Now you're creased—still "Hey, let's meet at the bay,"
Then you're timid—not cock sure of yourself,
Now you're aged—seen the fuller air and larger day.

39. Sing in rain and sing in shine

In the loft of my red brick terrace house,
I found an anachronistic piece of small history,
It was a mini Walkman music player.
Ballistically, I wiped the dust off with a soft cloth,
Its turquoise green skin burnished in a trice.

The past time seems to be once again
Lived on, those days in wind or rain;
On the way to my dwelling, under the dim light,
I was immersed in the melody of singing,
Forgot where I was, what the world was like.

I remembered singing, "It's all about in the winter"
Imagine no matter how cold and brittle the wind,
Forgive me, my dearest girl, I don't care
If I presented in you, ragged, bellowed,
That's cos I've crossed miles of arduous journey.

These beautiful songs played in my bygone days,
Still like yesterday's rain dropped on withered leaves.
I can smell its smell and feel the loom of the youth,
Amazed that as if my old dress still fit today's me,
With it, I dance by the brook under the starry night.

40. Spring in the garden

Spring in the garden,
Scissor-like wind ceased.
The sun shines on the wakening plants,
Majestic life restored, as you see
Lilies and tulips greet with vigorous blooming,
Spanish bluebells nod the night away.

Penstemons open their golden sleepy eye,
Daffodils dance in the morning breeze,
Japanese maple thickens its welcomed leaves;
Ruby azaleas stretch the warm embrace,
Magnolia petals covered silently by the morning dew,
Teeming grass painted by wildflowers with many hues.

Robin sits on the sweet gum branch in the mid air
And that's his branch never quitting for his return;
Blackbird goes into silver birch swaying lightly,
They sing to each other with their ardent voice.

Every morning they sing these beautiful songs
For they have a dawning chorus to broadcast.

And let's not forget my cat Mimi-
He spotted a cosy patch on the grass
Dozed his head away in a long-awaited dream.
The garden is my deepest soul's habitat -
In there I sow my hopes and fondness
Time flows, no return but love never fades.

41. Hello, spring

Hello, spring,
Embracing the much-loved undulating land
Grant the cold ground with generous warmth
Adorn the mountains and woods lush again.

Hello, spring,
Here she is to throw her magic wonder
Over the frozen lake, breathes her tender breath,
Let the lake ripple again with joy.

Smile to spring
With your sweet and amber light of lightness,
Blackbirds sing and roses charm
Myriad of daffodils dancing the night away.

42. My city at its indelible back

I walked along the quiet cobblestone path
At the back of bursting market street,
The golden afterglow of the sunset
Shines on the amber clock tower.
People call this city a dream of spires,
Its honey-colour domed buildings
Baptised in thousands of years of wind and rain,
Lived by countless imperishable souls and
Dedicated scholars, gave her indelible ink of life;
Genius minds, solitude thoughts, above all
Strong hearts, strive through good and bad days,
Walk into the future with grit and resolve.

The sound of church bell's jangle mingles with
My foot stepping, lingering in this like-no-other path.

43. To my city

The thousand-year-old town,
Every nook is enchanting.
Honey-coloured buildings
Blend ancient and modern;
The bustling high street
Is a road leading to the hall;
The gentle babbling river
Wings numerous rowing boats,
The sacred divine spires
Soaring into the heavenly clouds.
The wind sways willow wickers
A rustling sound round the courtyard;
Under the moon and stars
Wanderers loom out of the darkness.

44. Christmas tree

Every year at Christmas time
We set up a Christmas tree.
It was an old shy fellow,
We give it a fresh brush.
By the windows,
With the helping hands of children,
Together we dress it up lively with the
Treasures accumulated over the years.
A little hope of green clover,
A forgiveness of red clown,
And forget not the love of angels.

In this Christmas, I stand by
This lonely old fellow,
Single-handed I string up these little
Pendants, pleased to see
All the collections snuggled
One next to the other

64

In this happy festive day.
They light up and renew
The whole world of me,
Long gone memories lingered
Around the Christmas tree.

45. Those old days

It was a salty, filthy and stuffy day
Summer of nineteen sixty-nine
I was little and capered in my courtyard;
My mum was taken to the camp,
And my brother was idled away.

Cicadas screaming in the sycamore trees,
Across sparsely populated dusty square
I looked out, on the burning asphalt street.
An aged man hunched over his steps
With a broom in his hands, sweeping.

My play buddy warned me don't get close
To him, as he doesn't belong to our tier;
No one's allowed to know his fate,
Not you, not me, don't hunt for answer
Let him stagger away in this sweating air.

That autumn, my mother took me
And my brother to visit my father
Who lived up to the north-west.
There, hundreds of mountains straddle
Between us; we must take a train through.

The long green wagon seemed endless,
Passengers jostled dashing on board.
I stood in the aisle of a cramped carriage
Looking through the crooked luggage stack,
For the first time ever I felt so yearning.

Rows of poplar trees flying backwards,
Dwindling figures up and down in the
Distanced fields. The green engine hissed
Along the platform, I saw hundreds of faces
Starved, predatory faces in the senile or little children
Like high tide crashed to the slowly advancing train.

All they wanted was small change that
Can buy them a hot meal in the evening,
Or give their starving children a biscuit;
All these basic desires seemed too gaudy
Worthy of risking their lives on the blazed trails.

When the slit iron-bogey rebreathed, the ear-
Splitting whistle startled away those
Who were still lying on the cabin windows,
Some dropped off with empty hands,
Some ran away like cats that got their cream.

The clunking stock was rumbling through
The mountainous terrain, bored passengers
Slumbered on each other's shoulders,
Untiring kids, clumsy, zipped back their parents'
Pocket searching for some fruity treats.

My eyes travelled with the gloomy light
Outside the windows, beneath the clouds
I saw stark rocks wrenched up to the sky
Endeavoured to catch a slim gush of sunbeam
Which was blocked by the mighty stones.

On a blue-black cold evening in that late autumn,
I was hugged into my grandma's shrivelled bosom.
For the first time, in the dim light of sooted lamp,
I stared at her strange withered face, couldn't
Believe finally we met in this close of a day.

As the thread of twilight darkened, it was dinner time.
I remembered Grandma cooked two boiled eggs.
The mere precious left-over, she blew off
The heat, warmed my hands and face, in her dialect
Understood none, gesturing me to gobble them down.

Looked around the gloomy room, cluttered with
Peat-clogged sandals and sodden patched
Straw cloak. There was incessant beating sound
From the gravel yard at the side of the house,
It was my grandpa chopping the walnuts off the tree.

Next day there was a wedding ceremony, my uncle,
An oil nozzle factory worker married a lady who
Lost her three fingers in a mysterious pain.
She gazed at him with her glittering eyes, jiggling,
He holds her with his roughened hands.

The wedding guests were met, sat on the stones
Masticated a feast of meal served in terracotta plates.
Village hall filled with disparate tumultuous chants,
Smoky air blurred the visage of bride's face, hinder
From the good wishes by the high-spirited callers.

No thrushes sing as the sun is going down.
By the river of the gloomier hilly village,
I was in awe of watching the merrymaking children
Indulged in their self-invented catch-a-fish play,
Sound of mirth lingered around the babbling brook.

The silhouette of the distant mountains stands
Vainly visible under the star light, the silent wonder
Splits the broad earth and sky, occasionally
Crows call from the woods, mingled with a whine
Of dogs, filled my spirit with a certain pious fear.

The returning journey crammed with empty yarns.
Drawn and tired sable eyes from everyone around
Gauged with doubt and confusion, no longer
Held the exuberance and striving as I went. Like
A sombre piglet, I drooped and curled into a corner.

71

Many years later, I parted from old buddies
By space and belief. We scarcely encounter.
Glance back the dreary track, these old
Blurred memories like dried grass, withered
Lost in dusty air but seeded in my heart.

I had no Proust's madeleine cake, nor did I
Have Rexroth's poker chip; I travelled further away
From my stunningly uneventful past, and today
I dwell in my own place with my own day, never mind
The bird's song would ever be the same again.

46. Listen to the rain

When I was down and perplexed, I liked
To listen to the rain by the lotus pond,
The sound of raindrops on lotus petals
Like a gentle drumstick tapping on my heart.

When I was glum and felt lost, I liked
To listen to the rain walking on the hills,
The patter of drizzle spattered in the woods
Escort my thoughts flying over the misty ground.

Now, after all these years I'm weary, I like
To listen to the rain by my windows, all silent
Only the raindrops tapping on the roof, sounds
Like ethereal pixies greeting softly, "hello".

47. I met a man who wasn't there

I met a man who wasn't there
He's gone for nearly a century long,
His imperturbable smile still flares
In this once-warmed pastoral den.

Beside a daisies' bank at the wood's lane
Stands a fine English house of red brick
Built by this genius of multi-faceted man
Yet his legacy goes far beyond dwelled stick.

From a pride farm mistress of frenzied crowd
To a pristine innocence killed by various vile;
And thousands of pieces of timeless lyrics
Every masterpiece enlightens my wonder of doubt.

I met a man who wasn't there anymore, his
Blood and tears all founded into his works.

48. Meet the time as it seeks

Last night, he dreamed of going through
A dark tunnel, at the end, lay an array of drifted
Houses and trees, vaguely he recognised
It was his estranged hometown.

Moonlight dashed through the sleepy burgh,
Dark shadows mottled on the withered leaves.
Hefty footsteps sounded like melodious drums
Echoing at the verge of indistinct village.

He cannot see what it was, since his bleary sight
Blurred in this dusky mist, as if there was a grey flag
Floating in the dark wood under the leaden sky.
Time is coming, in this lonely unexpected night.

49. A mother's repentance

On a still morning at the end of the kitchen table,
She was planning an end-of-year family reunion,
Gnawing the hard crust of wholemeal bread.
With a burst of aurora tone, a message appears
On the phone screen; it's from her daughter.

"Dear Mother, the year's gone by so fast
You asked me to come home around this
Special time, But I don't think I can.
Dear Mother, I'm not saying I fell apart
Or am cowardly alienated away from you.

I just don't want to go back to my past
As it's like a dark thorny web once
Enveloped my freedom of breath,
Moulds my yearning heart into stiffness;
Either fly or being flung, or I'm worth nothing.

I remembered you and Father many
Times impatiently urged me to stumble
Away from breakfast table, treated me as
A family's shame by shouting "scallywag"
For I was once late for my morning chores.

You called me irresponsible, shallow, merely
Unworthy of naivety, pleasing to the honey
Words on other people's tip of tongues.
Oh, Mother, my heart yearned to be hugged
And loved by you, I keeled on the wrong side."

Thus far, tears fall on her wrinkled face,
Her eyes dazzled in great mist of sorrow;
Immense sense of penance in the lost
Time, she and her daughter could never
Be the same again, but can't she restart?

50. Ode to the spring

Spring knocking my windows, her fingers of
East breeze, softly wake me up, along with
My little hibernating floral frock, wear it on
To embrace the rejuvenation of the land;
The grass secretly drilled out of the soil,
The seemingly dead twigs sprout new buds
Tender and glint, the sun gushes through.

Looking around wild flower everywhere,
Various, has the name, has not the name,
Disperses in the teeming patch of grass,
Looks like the eyes, blue and white, twinkling.

The birds set their nests among flowers
And tender leaves, they cheer up
Showing off their crispy voice, singing melodies
Echoing the babbling water along the river Avon.

Rain falling in the sky, like ox hair or rabbit fur,
Each filament interwoven into a thin mist
Swirling around the hazy roof of the houses
Crisscrossing the wavy lines of tree and land.

Dogs run, children play, people chant,
Ducks swim, squirrels skulk, and worms dig;
Spring brings such vitality of life back to
The southern hemisphere, nature prevails.

Milton Keynes UK
Ingram Content Group UK Ltd.
UKHW041804131123
432470UK00022B/7